If the Battle is the Lord's... Why Am I So Tired?

Randy Newberry

RPJ & Co.
P.O. Box 160243
Altamonte Springs, Florida
32716-0243
rpjandco@yahoo.com

Front Cover Illustration:
Roohee Mirbaha

Graphic and Graphics Designs:
American Photos, Graphics and Designs
www.picturestoart.com

ISBN: 0-9761122-0-5

Printed in the United States of America

All scripture is quoted from the King James Version, unless otherwise noted.

Acknowledgements

I would first like to thank my wife Linda for her faithful encouragement and support in everything I do. I want also to thank Kathy Schubitz for all of the hours she put into making this book a reality. I would like to thank Pastor Betty Johnson of Sunshine Cathedral, Plant City, Florida, Apostle Nelia Frazier of Eagles Mount Fellowship & Prophetic Ministries Training Center in Riverview, Florida, and a very special thank you to Pastor Bobby Manning of God's House in Bradenton, Florida; for all of their prayers and support. I would also like to thank Pastor Paul and Pastor Isaac of AOB Missions in Bangalore, India and Pastor Todo Julien of Redemption Life Ministries of Haiti for the experiences in their countries that led to my writing this book, and to everyone else who touched my life.

God bless you all,

Randy

Table of Contents

vi

Introduction

Why are we so tired? It seems as if we are worn out. A vast majority of people, not just Christians, are disgusted, discouraged and defeated. There must be a reason or reasons why. Sometime ago the Lord gave me this title. For a long time I would just mention the title in my messages and the response would be very encouraging. But I really had not given the subject a whole lot of thought. Then it would come up more and more. So I finally decided that I would give it a shot. And here it is. I hope that you will find this attempt to bring some sort of balance to the body of Christ concerning spiritual warfare, and just plain everyday living, worthy of your time.

God Bless You,

Randy Newberry

1

The Warfare

David declared it in 1 Samuel 17:47, "*And all this assembly shall know that the Lord saveth not with sword and spear: for the battle is the Lord's, and he will give you into our hands.*" Of course, this particular battle is the epic battle of the Israelites and the Philistines. We know it as the story of David and Goliath, but it really was not just about David and Goliath. It is a graphic picture of the church. You see the Israelites on one mountain and the Philistines on another one and there was a valley between them.

Then the Philistines would send out their champion named Goliath, (whose name means splendor). He would challenge the Israelites every day for forty days. Forty is the number of temptation in scripture. Jesus was tempted forty days in the wilderness (Matthew 4:1). Every day the giant, Goliath, would issue a challenge to the Israelites to send out a man to fight against him. Whoever would win this fight, the other side would serve them. My first question is, why were they letting the enemy issue the challenge? Who is he to determine our battles or strategies?

It is no wonder to me when anyone but God is leading that we find ourselves in situations and circumstances beyond our control. No wonder we are so tired, frustrated, and discouraged! I have often wondered why so many people give up or burn out. Ministers quitting the ministry; people just giving up on life altogether; something must be wrong; not with God's plan, but perhaps our execution of it.

Thank God David shows up on the scene. He over hears this Giant challenging the people of God. David, representing our savior, accepts the challenge. David asks in verse 29 of Chapter 17 in 1 Samuel, "...Is there not a cause?" Sometimes the reason for our lack of determination to do what we know is right is our lack "of a cause." Our cause will keep us going. It will give us the unction to function. Maybe we just need to re-examine our "cause." David's "cause" gave him the backbone to stand against a giant. He took care of Goliath in short order. He had Faith that his God was more than able. If we really believe that our God is able, it will make our plight much easier.

There is also another place in scripture where this is repeated. It is the battle between Jehoshaphat and the Moabites, Ammonites, and the inhabitants of Mount Seir, in 2 Chronicles 20:15. The Spirit of the Lord came upon Jahaziel "And he said, Hearken ye, all Judah, and ye inhabitants of Jerusalem, and king Jehoshaphat, Thus saith the Lord unto you, be not afraid nor dismayed by reason of this great multitude; for the battle is not yours, but God's." Listen to verse 17, "Ye shall not need to fight in this battle: set yourselves, stand ye still, and see the salvation of the Lord with you, O Judah and Jerusalem: fear not, nor be dismayed; tomorrow go out against them: for the Lord will be with you." Verse 20 says, "And they rose early in the morning, and went forth into the wilderness of Tekoa: and as they went forth, Jehoshaphat stood and said, Hear me, O Judah and ye inhabitants of Jerusalem; Believe in the Lord your God, so shall ye be established; believe his prophets, so shall ye prosper." Verse 21: "And when he had consulted with the people, he appointed singers unto the Lord, and that should praise the beauty of holiness, as they went out before the army, and to say, Praise the Lord; for his mercy endureth for ever." Verse 22 says, "And when they began to sing and to praise, the Lord set ambushments against the children of Ammon, Moab, and Mount Seir, which were come against Judah; and they were smitten." There is one more verse that we must read, verse 25. "And when Jehoshaphat and his people came to take away the spoil of them, they found among them in abundance of riches with the dead bodies, and precious jewels, which they stripped off for themselves, more than they could carry away: and they were three days in gathering of the spoil, it was so much."

Now this is the way it is supposed to be. When the enemy comes against us, the people of God, the Lord fights the battle, and when we sing praise to God, we walk away with a blessing that is too much to carry.

What a way to do battle! I believe there is much to learn from this battle. The first thing they did was to seek the Lord for direction. Do not fight any battle without the word of the Lord. Secondly, he said believe in the Lord God, so shall ye be established. Established is what? The Lord. We must establish ourselves in Him. To be established means to be settled, settled in Him, not wavering. People should know where you stand with the Lord; that the Lord fights your battles. There should also be no question about your character; your character is being established.

Then he said to believe his prophets so shall ye prosper. I am well aware that not everyone who gives a word of prophecy is actually hearing from God. So it makes it hard sometimes to know what to believe. But I have learned from the book of Revelation 19:10 it says, *"...for testimony of Jesus is the Spirit of Prophecy."* In other words, the spirit will bear witness with the Christ in you. The word will be producing Christ in you, not just pleasing the flesh.

The third thing Jehoshaphat did was do exactly what God directed him to do. It did not seem like a good plan to the natural mind. Many times God's ways do not make sense to us, carnally. But God's ways are higher than man's ways. Because of his obedience, they not only won the battle, they were blessed beyond their wildest dreams. They were just fighting to stay alive. But God wanted them to have their lives and have them more abundantly. This sounds like the same plan that Jesus spoke about in John 10:10, *"The thief cometh not but for to steal, and to kill and to destroy: I am come that they might have life, and that they might have it more abundantly."*

The one thing I want to emphasize is when we are obedient to the plan of God, not only are we able to win our battles, but we do not wear ourselves out in the process. We also get the spoils from the battle. With God it is a win-win situation. I must point out this battle was also fought in a wilderness. The wilderness seems to be the place of many battles. The most important battles in scripture were fought in the wilderness. The Children of Israel wandered in the wilderness for forty years before entering into the promise land. A wilderness is a barren, empty, desert like place. Most of our more important battles in life are fought when we are going through rough places. Remember, these are the battles that determine our future or destiny. We really need to heed to the divine leadership of our Lord, in these times.

Another one of my favorite scriptures dealing with spiritual warfare is Psalm 68, verse 1, *"Let God arise, let his enemies be scattered: let them also that hate him flee before him."* You see when we let or allow God to arise within us, He takes his rightful place on the throne of our hearts. This means that He is calling the shots. He is making the decisions in our lives. The enemy has to flee. He cannot get in to put in his two cents. The

Apostle Paul says in Ephesians 4:27, *"Neither give place to the devil."* Give him no room in your life. Many people have a great big Devil and a very little God, or so it seems. All they can talk about is how Satan is fighting or how hard it is to live right. If our focus is on the enemy, he will be larger than life. If our focus is on God, then He will be larger than life. Which one do you want to be larger in your life?

We know that Christ in you is the hope of Glory according to Colossians 1:27. When we allow the hope to spread by letting Him arise, there really is no weapon formed against us that can prosper or gain ground in our lives (Isaiah 54:17) and every tongue that shall rise against thee in judgment thou shalt condemn, this is the heritage of the saints.

I really like the part about this being the heritage (or the inheritance) of the saints. We are the saints of God. These promises are for us, but we must activate them in our lives. How many times did Jesus say things like, *"If thou canst believe, all things are possible to him that believeth,"* (Mark 9:23) or John 14:12-14, *"Verily, verily, I say unto you, He that believeth on me, the works that I do shall he do also; and greater works than these shall he do; because I go unto my Father. And whatsoever ye shall ask in my name, that will I do, that the Father may be glorified in the Son. If ye shall ask any thing in my name, I will do it."* So you see, one of our greatest weapons is simply to believe.

Notice, He did not say those who fight the hardest or pray the loudest, or work the most hours will receive. No, He said those that believe. It is easier for us to work hard than for us to believe. Mostly because what we have to believe is not "carnally correct." By this I mean that it does not make sense to the carnal mind. But then Paul said in Romans 8:5-8, *"For they that are after the flesh do mind the things of the flesh, but they that are after the Spirit the things of the Spirit. For to be carnally minded is death; but to be spiritually minded is life and peace. Because the carnal mind is enmity against God: for it is not subject to the law of God, neither indeed can be. So then they that are in the flesh cannot please God."*

I do not know how much plainer it can be put. The carnal mind is enmity or the enemy of God. Yet we tend to want to reason everything with our carnal minds. God's ways are higher than man's ways. Just like the battle that we read about earlier, with Jehoshaphat; how many modern day battles have you heard about where they sent singers and praisers before the army? It does not make sense to us because we see through natural or carnal eyes. Obviously, God has his reasons. Maybe the warfare was won by the praisers and singers before the natural army arrived on the scene!

I wonder how many times praising was the plan of God in our everyday warfare against our enemies, but we were too busy to consult God first, or if we did, we were too embarrassed to do it. We think, "we can handle this one God, you take a break. I'll show you how capable I am," only to find ourselves in a bigger mess than ever. We need God's help, always in everything we do, whether it seems spiritual or not. Many times we wear ourselves out trying to impress others. If we could forget about trying to impress everyone else and only try to please God, the battle would not be nearly as difficult. Remember the battle is the Lord's!

2

Weapons of Our Warfare

Paul says in 2 Corinthians, chapter 10, verses 3-6, *"For though we walk in the flesh, we do not war after the flesh: (For the weapons of our warfare are not carnal, but mighty through God to the pulling down of strongholds); Casting down imaginations, and every high thing that exalteth itself against the knowledge of God and bringing into captivity every thought to the obedience of Christ; And having in a readiness to revenge all disobedience, when your obedience is fulfilled."*

Once again, we are reminded in scripture that our warfare is not after the flesh, or done by the flesh. We cannot do spiritual battle with carnal minds. He said the weapons of our warfare are mighty through God. What are the weapons? Ephesians 6:10-18 gives us a list of the weapons and the armour or protection that we need for this battle. The reason we must take the time to go over these scriptures is because of the vital importance they are to our everyday walk in Christ.

Verse 10 says, *"Finally, my brethren, be strong in the Lord, and in the power of his might,"* not our might. *Put* on the whole armour of God, that ye may be able to stand against the wiles of the devil. For we wrestle not against flesh and blood, but against principalities, against powers, against the rulers of the darkness of this world, against spiritual wickedness in high places. Wherefore take unto you the whole armour of God, that ye may be able to withstand in the evil day, and having done all, to stand. Stand therefore, having your loins girt about with truth, and having on the breastplate of righteousness; And your feet shod with the preparation of the gospel of peace; Above all, taking the shield of faith, wherewith ye shall be able to quench the fiery darts of the wicked. And take the helmet of salvation, and the sword of the Spirit, which is the word of God: Praying always with all prayer and supplication in the Spirit and watching thereunto with all perseverance and supplication for all saints..."

Now let us go back and examine what Apostle Paul was instructing us to do. First, he said to be strong in the Lord and in the power of his might. We must understand that our strength is not of ourselves. Paul says in 2 Corinthians 12:10, "....for when I am weak, then am I strong." He also said in verse 9 of the same chapter, "And he said unto me, my grace is sufficient for thee: For my strength is made perfect in weakness." Jesus is the one saying this. His strength is made perfect in our weakness. Our strength is in Him and in His might, not our own.

Then he says to put on the whole armour of God.

The armour of God is a protective covering against the enemies' attacks. Remember earlier we read of David and Goliath, when David convinced Saul to let him go to fight the Giant, Saul told him to try on his armour. When David did this, he found it to be too big, it just did not feel right. Many times we try to put on someone else's armour. What I mean by this is, is asking someone else what to do in certain situations, and not asking the Lord for ourselves. What someone else would do may be good for them but God might have you do something else. For instance, I may be going through something that my wife Linda has gone through before. So I would ask her what she did at that time. She may tell me that she fasted and prayed for three days, but when I tried it all I got was hungry, because I did not seek the Lord. Her advice was good, but it did not work for me. Saul's armour was good but it did not work for David.

Then Paul says to *"put on the whole armour of God, that ye may be able to stand against the wiles of the devil,"* (Ephesians 6:10) or the attacks of the devil. The Amplified Bible says *"against all the strategies and deceits of the devil."* He then says that our warfare is not against flesh and blood but against principalities. The first thing that comes to my mind when I hear the word principalities is the word principles. Principles are the fundamentals. Fundamentals of our faith many times are shaky, especially when so many Christians today are being raised on emotions rather than true spiritual principles. Jesus taught many Kingdom principles throughout the four gospels.

In fact, he was speaking of this very thing in Matthew 7:24-27. *"Therefore whosoever heareth these sayings of mine, and doeth them, I will liken him unto a wise man, which built his house upon a rock: And the rain descended, and the floods came, and the winds blew, and beat upon that house; and it fell not: for it was founded upon a rock. And every one that heareth these sayings of mine, and doeth them not, shall be likened unto a foolish man, which built his house upon the sand: And the rain descended, and the floods came, and the winds blew, and beat upon that house; and it fell: and great was the fall of it."*

When the storms of life come we need to know that we have built our lives on solid spiritual principles so our lives will not fill apart. Sadly to say our hospitals, prisons, even Asylums are full of people who did not heed the word of the Lord. Many of our homes, even in the church are falling apart because of a lack of a solid foundation. Jesus is our foundation. Not even the church can take the place of a real relationship with Him.

Much of our battle is in the mind. Mental fatigue is one result of the battle within the mind, without proper principles in place. Our basic principles are really, "what we believe" and this is what determines our success or failure in life. I am not writing this just so we can be better church members. My goal is to help us be more effective in life and have more joy. If the church is where it should be, then it can truly be a light to those who are trying to find their way. It is kind of like trying to make a child grow; all you really have to do is keep him healthy, he will grow. The same thing works for the church or a relationship; keep them healthy and they will grow.

Now back to the scriptures at hand. Principalities also refer to demonic forces. We know that our enemy is a liar and the father of lies. Every thought that he puts in our mind is a lie, or based on a lie. If it appears to be true it is being misused. He will not speak truth. He cannot handle the truth. The truth will expose him, so he must use deceit and lies.

Not only do we wrestle against principalities but powers and against rulers of darkness in this world. Powers in this particular use makes me think of the ability of one person having control over another. This also can be demonic or it can simply be a form of manipulation. We know that manipulation is actually a form of witchcraft. It can also be as simple as depending too much on what someone else thinks. The need to please sometimes puts us under a sort of spell. If I care too much about what someone else thinks they can have power over me. For example, if I know that I should speak to someone about Jesus but I am afraid they might laugh or think something bad about me, then they have too much power over me. You may not even know it, but I am giving you that power by caring more about your feelings than I do about being obedient to God. We must care more about pleasing God than man, even our own selves.

The rulers of darkness are those who have power to impart evil. Once again, it can be demonic, but it can also be fear, doubt, or unbelief. These things can bring much darkness to someone's life. Many times, people spread darkness by planting seeds of doubt or unbelief in the mind of another. For instance, I have heard of a famous body builder who would see his opponent before a contest and ask him if he was feeling alright. He may remark that he looked a little pale. When in reality it was just a ploy, but if the opponent would listen to this remark it would affect his performance and give the other person an edge over him. It works the same with negative influence. Just being around someone who is negative will make you the same way if you are not careful. Many times the perpetrators do not even realize what they are doing.

We must move on to the weapons. The first thing He says to do, is stand. We have heard it said that a person who will not stand for something will fall for anything. I believe the Apostle Paul is telling us to take a stand for God. Stand with your loins girt about with truth. The truth will make you free! There is so much that we could say about Truth. *Jesus is the way, the truth, and the life* (John 14:6). The truth will stand and it will make you able to stand.

Then he said to have on the breastplate of righteousness. We know the breastplate covers the chest area, and this is where all of the vital organs are, such as the heart. Having on the breastplate is having our heart right with God. Our righteousness is with God and not in our own works. Righteousness means to be in right standing.

Having your Feet shod with the preparation of the gospel of peace, speaks of being prepared or ready to speak peace in any situation that warrants it. The shield of faith protects against the fiery darts of the wicked. Many books have been written on faith. I was just reminded of one verse in Hebrews 11:6 that says, *"But without faith it is impossible to please him: for he that cometh to God must believe that he is, and that he is a rewarder of them that diligently seek him."* When our faith is in tact, there is really not much the enemy can do to us. This is why our Faith is constantly being attacked. Do not give in; keep the faith. Faith will move mountains and it will move God!

Next is the helmet of salvation. Of course, the helmet is the protection for the head, or the mind. We have the mind of Christ according to 1 Corinthians 2:16. It is in the mind that we know things--things like, we are called to be Sons of God. If the enemy can get us to doubt our identity in Christ then he can rob us of our blessings and have his way in us. The helmet of Salvation is knowing, knowing your relationship with God. Hosea 4:6 says, *"My people are destroyed for lack of knowledge: because thou hast rejected knowledge, I will also reject thee..."* This is why this piece of armour is so important. The lack of knowledge is destroying many people by not knowing who they are in Christ, not knowing their place in His body, the church. They say that knowledge is power. Know your God, the more you know the truth about God, the more you will want to serve Him.

He then says to take the sword of the Spirit which is the word of God. This really is your only weapon that you have. This is why it is so important to know the word of God, not just the written word. We can never know too much scripture, but we also must understand that Jesus is the Word of God made Flesh (John 1:14). Knowing him is knowing the living word. Knowing His voice will drastically reduce the risk of falling or being led astray. He said my sheep know my voice, a stranger they will not follow (John 10:4-5). The only way to know someone is to spend time with them. We must spend time with God, not just telling Him our troubles but listening to His voice in our hearts. Paul also says in Philippians 3:10, *"That I may know him, and the power of his resurrection, and the fellowship of his sufferings, being made conformable unto his death."* This is really knowing Him. Many want to know Him in the power of his resurrection but what about the fellowship or His sufferings? It has been said that you really do not know someone until you have been through some rough times together. Staying with Jesus through hard times will prove rewarding.

I remember my first trip out of the United States. I was going to India to minister. I had never flown in an airplane and I was to be gone for sixteen days. My wife, Linda and I had never been apart that long, during our marriage of thirty years. In addition, I was going to a foreign country alone! I really had to trust God. I prayed like I had never prayed before. I learned to lean on Him in ways I had never thought of before. I was to minister to thousands and had never preached with an interpreter before. I faced fears that I did not know I had. Do you know what? God was faithful in every way! The more I leaned on Him, the more I found Him to be worthy of my trust. God is faithful, and I know Him now, like I had never known Him before.

You may be thinking this is all well and good but how does this help me as a weapon, a sword. You see, the greatest battle is really in the mind. When you know the word of the Lord you can fight back any attacks that come your way. You can quote scripture, and you can dismantle any lies that come against you by knowing you have a word from God. Let's look at 2 Timothy 2:15, it says to *"Study to shew thyself approved unto God, a workman that needeth not to be ashamed, rightly dividing the word of truth."* Many times when we read this scripture we think He is saying that the more we study the more we will be approved. And I am not arguing against this, but I think He is also telling us when we study, we should be finding out that we are approved! Not by our works, but by His works.

Now, I am not saying that we should not study. I am saying when we study that we should be really hearing what the Lord is saying to us, not necessarily what we have always been told. He also says in 2 Timothy 3:16 that *"All scripture is given by inspiration of God, and is profitable for doctrine, (teaching) for reproof, for correction, for instruction in righteousness: That the man of God may be perfect, throughly furnished unto all good works."* The word of God is good for us. It will make us perfect or mature in Him. This is the real goal anyway. Many times the word is used to beat ourselves up or beat up others. The word is a sword or weapon to use on the enemy, not on ourselves for destruction or on our brothers and sisters. We are not even to use it to destroy people out in the world. We should use it to build up one another, to encourage, and to strengthen.

"For the word of God is quick, (alive) and powerful, and sharper than any two-edged sword, piercing even to the dividing asunder of soul and spirit, and of the joints and marrow, and is a discerner of the thoughts and intents of the heart" (Hebrews 4:12).

You see, the word of God is a mighty weapon and

it must be used correctly. Too much damage has already been done by well-meaning Christians using this powerful weapon. The word of God should only be used on others as you would use it on yourself. In fact, use it on yourself first, then you probably will not have to use it on anyone else!

The Wrong War

Another reason we are so tired is because we are fighting battles that are not even ours to fight, or even worse, we are fighting battles that have already been won. You see, understanding what Jesus has already done for us would really help us a whole lot!

Let us go to Isaiah 53:4, Isaiah prophesying about Jesus' suffering said, *"Surely he hath borne our griefs and carried our sorrows: yet we did esteem him stricken, smitten of God, and afflicted. But he was wounded for our transgressions, he was bruised for our iniquities: the chastisement of our peace was upon him; and with his stripes we are healed."* I really do not want to get into a doctrinal dispute over healing, mostly because it is not the reason for this particular writing. It is easy for someone when they are well to say to someone sick, "if you had enough faith you could be healed." Of course, when that same person gets sick, it is a different story.

What I would like to say is we need to be more like the three Hebrew children in the book of Daniel. When they were thrown into the fire, their attitude was that they knew their God was able to deliver them but even if he didn't, they would not bow to any other Gods.

I certainly believe God can heal, but if I do not get healed, I am not going to beat myself up over not having enough faith! We must rest in the fact that He can if He chooses but if He does not, I am still going to serve Him to the best of my ability. The same can be said for any other situation. Many people are wearing themselves out trying to work their way to heaven or into good standing with God. I believe we should work for the Lord. James 2:17-18 says, *"Even so faith, if it hath not works, is dead, being alone. Yea, a man may say, Thou hast faith, and I have works: show me thy faith without thy works, and I will shew thee my faith by my works."*

In other words, you cannot have true faith without works but you also cannot work your way into God's good grace. James 1:22 also says, *"But be ye doers of the word and not hearers only, deceiving your own selves."* The key here is to be a doer of God's word and not of man made doctrines. It is a good thing to go to church but we can get so caught up in going to church that we sometimes forget we "are" the church. We really do not have to go anywhere. Assembling ourselves together is needful but when it becomes ritualistic or legalistic it loses its value. Some people cannot get to church but they will not lose their salvation over it. If you can go to church, just do it. Everything we do, we need to do because we want to, because we love the Lord, not because we have to.

Many people are still trying to battle against sin. Please hear me out before you close the book. I will be the first to admit that I have not reached perfection, but the sin problem was dealt with at Calvary. Jesus died for our sins! We read about it in Isaiah. I am not saying that we do not mess up, but I am saying Jesus died for my sin, past, present, and future. There will never be another sufficient sacrifice for sin. The sin debt has been paid. I am not just a sinner saved by grace; I am a child of God! I am not trying to do good enough for my Father to accept me; He accepted me when I was born, even before I was born. He took care of the sin issue when he died on the cross. I am no longer to be sin-conscious. You see, if I am constantly focused on my sin, then I am going to be battling with sin. 2 Corinthians 5:21 says *"For he hath made him to be sin for us, who knew no sin; that we might be made the righteousness of God in him."*

I have been made the righteousness of God in Christ! My focus should be on Christ. If this is true I will not be worrying about sin; I will be concerned about those things that concern Him. I do not have to try to earn my Father's love. He loved me before I knew Him. We love Him because He first loved us. God is Love. This is His nature. He will never love us any more than He does right now, and He will never love us any less. We work for Him because we are saved, not to get saved.

I really do not like to use the term work because if it is a joy then it is not really work, is it?

I am reminded of the scripture in Galatians 2, verses 20 and 21, *"I am crucified with Christ: nevertheless I live; yet not I, but Christ liveth in me: and the life which I now live in the flesh I live by the faith of the Son of God, who loved me, and gave himself for me. I do not frustrate the grace of God: for if righteousness come by the law, then Christ is dead in vain."* When you first read this scripture you probably would not think that this verse has any relevance to us. We are not trying to live by the old testament Law, but it does not have to be the old Law, it can be any man made law, that brings us under bondage. You see, it is not Christ plus the law; it is just Christ. We should want to live right and if our heart is really right, we will live right, but not because of a law. It is very easy to want to go back to living under the law.

The truth is, our life is really not about us, it is about Jesus Christ! This verse says we are crucified with Christ, it is Him living through us. It is His desires that matter, not mine. I may still be walking around breathing air and doing everyday chores, but I do not live for myself, but Him. We are new creatures created in Christ Jesus. Paul says that I do not frustrate the grace of God. How do we frustrate the grace of God? By going back to the Law of sin and death, by giving in to our fleshly desires or simply trying to please God by our works. Verse 2 of chapter three says *"This only would I learn of you, received ye the Spirit by the works of the Law or by healing of faith."* In other words, works of the flesh did not get us saved and will not keep us saved. We are saved by faith and we are kept by faith. What I am trying to say is that we need not to worry and fret about our salvation. Just enjoy it! If you have accepted Christ as your savior, you are saved. If not, then do it; it is not that complicated. The Christian life is not as hard as we try to make it.

Let's look at Romans 8:35-39. *"Who shall separate us from the Love of Christ? Shall tribulation, or distress, or persecution, or famine, or nakedness, or peril, or sword? As it is written, For thy sake we are killed all the day long, we are accounted as sheep for the slaughter, nay in all things we are more than conquerors through him that loved us, For I am persuaded, that neither death nor life, nor angels, nor principalities, nor powers, nor things present, nor things to come, shall be able to separate us from the love of God, which is in Christ Jesus our Lord."*

It sounds like Apostle Paul is convinced that nothing will separate us from the love of God. He said we are more than conquerors through Jesus Christ, in all things. If we can get this settled in our hearts and in our minds, we would save ourselves a whole lot of worry. Think about it, persecution, famine, nakedness, peril. These are pretty serious things. Then He said, not even death, or life, things present or anything that might come our way in the future. Nothing shall separate us! He did not say if we are persuaded, those things would not separate us. He said He was persuaded that they would not separate us. He does not even know us, but he did know his God. His confidence is not in us, but in His God. This is awesome! If it is true, why do we worry so much?

Before everyone gets upset at me, I did not say you cannot turn away from God. I said trust God and He will not turn His back on you. None of these things will stop Him from loving us. If He can love us through all of this, then surely we can love Him.

One more thing on this 'more than conquerors' idea--you cannot be declared a winner until the battle is over, right? But we have already been crowned victorious, winners, conquers. Do you think maybe he knows something we do not? I have said many times that it makes a fight more exciting if you know before hand that you are going to win. This is the case in this battle of life. So remember, tomorrow when it seems like all of hell is attacking you, the fight is fixed. If you will just keep your trust in Him, you will win.

War in Peace

I mentioned earlier about my trip to India. While I was on this trip, God spoke something to my spirit that I know really helped me in this area of resting in the Lord. First, let me set the stage. I had flown for over thirty two hours including layovers. When I arrived there, my two Indian brothers met me at the airport. They greeted me and told me how glad they were to see me and we would be having service in a few hours. Now, I do want to say they took very good care of me, but we had a lot to do and a really short time to do it in. They had asked me to help them oversee their twenty seven churches.

So my purpose for going was not for big crusades; my primary purpose was to visit the churches. And that is exactly what we did. Twenty seven churches in less than 12 days! We traveled all over South India.

One night after service, they told me to bring my bags because we were going to take a train ride to the next meeting place. We rode for twelve hours, all night. I could not sleep. I could not eat the food; again, this was not their fault. We were in this place for 3 days and we took another 12 hour train ride. By this time, I was beginning to get sick to my stomach. For those who have never been to India, they do not have toilets, at least not like ours. But it was on this second trip, about halfway to our next destination when the Lord began speaking something to me. Of all things He could say to me, He spoke I Timothy 6:6 into my spirit. It says, *"but godliness with contentment is great gain."*

I immediately thought it was a rebuke. Since I was rapidly becoming disillusioned about this missionary business, I had begun to wonder if perhaps God was mad at me. Here I am in this strange land, literally sick and tired; I guess I was feeling a little like David in Psalm 137, when he was being carried away captive and his enemies asked him if he could sing the songs of Zion. And he asked how can he sing the Lord's song in a strange land. In the midst of all this, this verse keeps going over and over in my spirit. *"Godliness with contentment is great gain."* Needless to say by this time I was not a happy camper, and this was not what I wanted to hear. So then I tried to reason with God. "I am really trying hard to be content. This was more your idea, Lord, than mine." It seemed as if the Lord was not listening to me. He just kept saying the same thing to me over and over, *"Godliness with contentment is great gain."*

Finally, after several hours of trying to argue my

case with God, I gave in. "Obviously, I am missing something, God! What are you trying to tell me, that godliness with contentment is great gain?" I heard it that time, like I had not heard it before. I began to understand what He was saying to me.

He was not mad at me; He was trying to tell me that Godliness or God-likeness is the focus of the verse. Contentment will come when I am living a godly life. I had always concentrated on the contentment part and worked at being content. He was telling me to be content to be like God would have me to be. He would bring contentment. You might be thinking, how could anyone be like God? But the truth is we were created in God's own image and likeness. We have really worked hard at not being like God. If we could learn to listen, to trust the inner voice of God, we would find it is not as hard as we have imagined it to be. We are influenced so much by T.V. advertisements, the news media, and peer pressure. Other people's opinions have more effect on us than we would like to admit. The thing God was telling me was that I need to rest in the goodness of God and He would bring true contentment into my life, even in a strange land!

Paul tells us in Hebrews 4:1-3 *"Let us therefore fear, lest a promise being left us of entering into his rest, any of you should seem to come short of it. For unto us was the gospel preached, as well as unto them: but the word preached did not profit them, not being mixed with faith in them that heard it. For we which have believed do enter into rest, as he said, As I have sworn in my wrath, if they shall enter into my rest: although the works were finished from the foundation of the world."*

Then he says in verse 10 of the same chapter, *"For he that is entered into his rest, he also hath ceased from his own works as God did from his."*

You see, there is a place in God that is a place of rest. Not just over yonder, but right here, now, in Jesus Christ. But you can not get there by your own works. He said you must cease from your own works. This is the promise land, so much of our frustration comes from putting everything off until some day after while. I am not saying that there is not more after this life. I am excited about what I believe is to come, but I am also excited about what is available right now!

He said in verse three, that we just read, we which have believed do (presently) enter into my rest. Some did not enter in because of unbelief, just like the children of Israel did not enter in, because of unbelief and the hardness of their hearts. Unbelief is keeping many people from entering in, even now. I am talking about church people who really have not found a place of rest in Jesus. I certainly hope they do in the next life, but why not now, in this life?

We must tell our minds to shut up, tune out the

influence of well meaning friends, quit letting the T.V. dangle things in front of us, telling us that if we had this car or wore these clothes we would be better off. Then, in order for us to have that car, or those clothes, we have to work more. Then because we have worked more, we have earned the right to have more credit which affords us the ability to get further in debt. Then we have to work more to pay the debt. By this time, that car is old, the clothes are worn out, and you have to start all over again. Is that being better off? I'm getting tired just thinking about it.

The truth is, this is how most of us in the western culture have accepted life, as how it is supposed to be. And we wonder why we are so tired and unfulfilled; the answer to our dilemma is not in things. Remember Jesus' words in Luke 12:15, *"And he said unto them, Take heed, and beware of covetousness: for a man's life consisteth not in the abundance of the things which he possesseth.* Verse 31 says, *"But rather seek ye the kingdom of God; and all these things shall be added unto you."* You see, He is not against us having things. It is looking to things to fill our life's real needs that is wrong. We were created with a need for God and nothing else will satisfy that need. Whether it be illicit sex, drugs, alcohol, or just staying busy with seemingly good things, nothing will take the place of a real relationship with Jesus!

One reason why Jesus was so hard on the religious crowd in His day was not because everything they did was bad, it was mostly because what they did was out of duty and not out of love.   They were doing it to please fleshly desires.   They wanted to appease God, not to please God. And when the day was done, they were tired and God was still not pleased. Sound familiar? So in order to do better, they would add more works, require more sacrifices, and still to no avail. When will we ever learn?   It is still not too late. Many may think so, but we are still breathing, there is still today, let's do it! Seek the Kingdom of God first; ask for God's opinion, and do not worry so much about the opinions of others.

5

War and Fear

Timothy 1:7, *"For God hath not given us the spirit of fear but of power and of love, and of a sound mind."* I am really amazed at the fear most people have today; they are afraid of everything. I spoke earlier of some of my fears in going to India, but God gave me grace to face my fears; I am eternally grateful. The biggest fear was the unknown. I believe this is true for a lot of people. They do not put their trust in God. So there is really nothing else out there to bring comfort. If I did not have faith to believe that God was in charge, and trust what is unknown to me is known to Him, I would really have some major concerns about what is going on in this world.

But I have talked with God. I have read His word; He has assured me there is no reason to worry. He has everything under control. I did not say that there was no reason to pray. Worrying does not help; prayer does. The secular media does not want you to rest in God. They could not sell as many newspapers. People would not watch as much news. Sensationalizing sells but it also brings unrest, instability and no peace. Once again,

I am not telling you that nothing bad is ever going to happen. The Bible says that it rains on the just as well as the unjust.   I am just saying your worrying is not going to change anything, but your faith and prayers will. He said that He did not give us the spirit of fear, but He gave us the spirit of power, the spirit of love, and the spirit of a sound mind. The Amplified Bible says that God did not give us the spirit of timidity (of cowardice, of craven and cringing and fawning fear) but He has given us a spirit of power and of love and of a calm and well-balanced mind and discipline and self-control. This sounds exactly like what is needed, a spirit from God for self-control. Wouldn't that calm a lot of spirits? God does not really intend for man to be troubled about everything. He said *"Casting your care upon him for he careth for you"* (1 Peter 5:7). He is able to bring peace in the midst of the storm.

Not long ago I was in the small nation of Haiti with a preacher friend of mine and another Haitian pastor. While we were there, we experienced tremendous unrest in that country. The Haitians were in the process of overthrowing the government and ousting the president. Well, one night while coming home from a service in the mountains, we were literally ambushed by some of the presidents' secret police. They came running out of the woods shooting their guns, forcing us to stop. The secret police ran up to the van we were in, with their guns pointed at our heads, ready to shoot. You see, they must have thought we were part of the rebels going to Port-au-Prince to help overthrow the President. We were traveling with a truck load (probably 30 people or more) in a pick-up truck.

The van we were in was loaded down with people. I am sure they thought we were up to no good. But the only weapons we had were the sword of the Lord (our bibles) and a few horns (saxophones and trumpets). Just before they were going to shoot us, the pastor in the back of the van spoke up and told them who he was and what we were doing. Thank God, one of the guys with the guns recognized the preacher and ordered the men not to shoot, and told them we were OK and to let us go. I must tell you I was greatly relieved, to say the least. Now if I were to tell you that I was not afraid would be a lie, but I can say I knew God was with us, and it was God that delivered us. The chances of that man knowing our Pastor friend were almost none, but God made sure we were safe in the midst of the storm.

I am reminded of when the disciples were in the boat and the storm came; Jesus was asleep in the back of the boat; the boat was being tossed by the wind and the waves (Matthew 8:23- 27). The disciples got scared and woke Jesus up. The first thing Jesus did is ask his disciples, *"why are ye fearful, O ye of little faith?"* Then he rebuked the winds and the sea and there was a great calm. I do not believe he was upset because they woke him; I believe he was concerned because they did not do what He did. They had the same power; He had already told them of the power that they had in His name.

It has been 2000 years and this same power has been available to us all along, and we still are not using it, partially because we do not understand how to use the name of Jesus. Anything done in the name must be done in the nature of Jesus, because the name means nature. In other words, if you speak the name of Jesus, but do not operate in His nature you will not see anything happen. The nature of Jesus is meekness, kindness, love, peace, and joy. You will find a list of the fruit of the spirit in Galatians 5:22-23. The manifested fruit are the evidence of the spirit working.

I know many people will get upset at me now, but please listen to me. You can imitate the gifts but you will not be able to imitate the fruit. You are either meek or you are not. You may fool people for a little while, but the truth will come out. Now I do believe we can speak to natural storms and have the same results Jesus did, if we believe, but I am more concerned that we learn to use this same principle for our spiritual storms.

The only problem is if you do not have peace, you cannot bring peace, or speak peace into anything. But a person who has peace in their heart can speak peace into a certain situation and expect to see results.

Many times Jesus said to "fear not" in Luke 12:32,

he said *"Fear not, little flock; for it is the Father's good pleasure to give you the kingdom."* Fear is really faith in evil instead of faith in God. 1 John 4:18 says, *"There is no fear in love; but perfect love casteth out fear: because fear hath torment. He that feareth is not made perfect in love."* So if perfect love casts out fear then our goal is to walk in perfect love which we know is found only in Jesus Christ. So the more we walk in Him and abide in Him, the more our love will be made perfect and fear will be overcome. Then we will be at peace and we can bring peace with us wherever we go. Isaiah 26:3 says *"Thou wilt keep him in perfect peace, whose mind is stayed on thee: because he trusteth in thee."*

Since this is the topic of this chapter, I would like to explore this peace a little more. Isaiah is telling us that God will keep us in perfect peace, if our mind is stayed or fixed on him (God). Then how can we fix our mind on Him?

Reading from the Amplified, it says *"You will guard him and keep him in perfect and constant peace whose mind (both its inclination and its character) is stayed on You, because he commits himself to you, leans on You and hopes confidently in you."* The next verse says *"So trust in the Lord (commit yourself to him, lean on him, hope confidently in him), forever, for the Lord God is an everlasting Rock (the Rock of Ages)."* God is committed to keep us in peace if we will commit ourselves to Him.

Commitment is not a popular word. In an age where people will not commit to each other in marriage or in anything else for that matter, and if they do, it is with stipulations. God's only stipulation is that we fix ourselves on Him. He said He would do the keeping; He will be your guide through this maze of life. If you fall, He will lift you up and He will give you peace. Philippians 4:7 says *"And the peace of God, which passeth all understanding, shall keep your hearts and minds through Christ Jesus."*

There is a peace which passes understanding, a peace that goes beyond your human intellect. You will never realize with your natural mind the peace that comes from God, and you can only get it from God. He said this peace is what keeps your heart and mind; keeps it from being tormented by the unknown; keeps it from being terrorized by the enemy.

There have been times in my Christian walk when I knew it had to be God that kept me from literally losing my mind. The pressures of this life can be overwhelming. But I knew in all the confusion I was going to come out alright, not by looking at outward circumstances, but by looking unto the Author and Finisher of my faith (Hebrews 11:6). I knew my God was able. I want to look at one more verse on peace. It is found in Colossians 3:15, *"And let the peace of God rule in your hearts, to the which also ye are called in one body; and be ye thankful."* Once we have learned to let the peace of God rule, we will be able to walk in a new dimension in God.

I am still learning how to do this. I have found before making decisions to pause, if not but for a moment, and see if I have a peace about my decision. If I do not have peace in my spirit, I do not do it, or at least I will wait until I get peace. I may not even know why at the time, but I have found it pays to let the peace of God rule. Do not let anybody steal your peace. People will try to force you to make decisions before you are ready. Do not do it. I do not always need a reason, but I always need peace.

War and the Kingdom

J esus said in Matthew 11:28-30 *"Come unto me, all ye that labour and are heavy laden, and I will give you rest. Take my yoke upon you, and learn of me, for I am meek and lowly in heart: and ye shall find rest unto your souls. For my yoke is easy, and my burden is light."* This sounds like a nobrainer. Jesus is willing to take your burden and give you a yoke that is easy and light. Many people are laboring and their burdens truly are heavy and they really could use some rest. Jesus is offering us the deal of a lifetime!

Why carry a load if you do not have to? The first requirement in this verse is to "come unto me." Of course, we know this is not literal but in our spirit, we have to approach Jesus. Enter into his presence. Psalm 100, verse 4 tells us to *"Enter into His gates with thanksgiving and into His courts with praise."* We use this verse in church for praise and worship, but it is a good way to come to Jesus anytime. Just begin to thank Him and praise Him. You will soon begin to realize His presence around you.

You see, you really do not have to pray Jesus down from heaven; He lives in you. As you worship Him, He is being released from within you. As He manifests Himself to you, whether it be through a peaceful calm coming over you or a goose bump experience, just enjoy His presence, enter His rest. Then release your burdens; you can tell Him about them if you want, but you really do not have to; He knows.

Then He says to take His yoke upon you, *"for my yoke is easy and my burden is light."* Trade Him burdens; give Him yours and ask Him what can I do for you, Lord? Then just wait for His answer; you will probably be surprised at what He says. I have had Him just show me somebody and say, pray for him or speak a kind word to them. It usually is not a big thing, but it gets your mind off your problems and shows the love of God to someone else. Now, I am not saying this is always how it happens, but you will find that taking your focus off of you and your problems and getting your attention on someone else, will work wonders.

One other thing He said in this verse that we miss a lot of times is to "learn of me." Matthew 11:29 says *"Take my yoke upon you and learn of me."* When we are obeying the word of the Lord and putting into practice Godly principles, we will learn things about God. He will reveal himself to us and even through us in ways that will amaze us. It really is a joy to learn of the Lord. This brings me to our next topic, Joy.

In Nehemiah 8:10 the last part of the verse says the *"joy of the Lord is your strength."* Now someone pointed out recently that it does not say your joy is the strength of the Lord. It is, His joy is your strength. So what is the joy of the Lord? Going back to the text in Nehemiah, they had just finished building the wall around Jerusalem. They had taken a day to read the book of the law. After reading the book of the law, they must have been saddened, probably much like many churches today that are constantly preaching law. The whole reason for the law was to show us that we could not keep it. When we are reminded of this, it brings sadness, but we are not left in that state.

The Apostle Paul tells us in Romans Chapter 8 beginning in verses 1-3, *"There is therefore now no condemnation (from the law) to them which are in Christ Jesus, who walk not after the flesh, but after the spirit. For the law of the spirit of the life in Christ Jesus hath made me free from the law of sin and death (the old law). For what the law could not do, in that it was weak through the flesh, God sending his own Son in the likeness of sinful flesh, and for sin, condemned sin in the flesh:"*

So God through his son took care of sin and the condemnation it brings, and has made a way for us to enter into the joy of the Lord. Jesus told the man in Matthew 25:21, who had been faithful with the talents that his master had given him. *"His lord said unto him, Well done, thou good and faithful servant: thou hast been faithful over a few things, I will make thee ruler over many things: enter thou into the joy of the Lord."* Paul also says in Romans 14:17 *"For the kingdom of God is not meat and drink; but righteousness, and peace, and joy in the Holy Ghost."* This next verse rarely ever read with it says, *"For he that in these things serveth Christ is acceptable to God, and approved of men."*

The joy of the Lord is a part of the Kingdom of God. So by receiving the joy of the Lord, we are receiving the Kingdom of God, and by operating in joy we are operating in the Kingdom of God, and God is well pleased. Getting back to Nehemiah; many people go to church, hear the law preached, condemnation sets in, then discouragement. It is no wonder there are so many defeated Christians, and so many people who do not want to have anything to do with church. If this was all there was to it, we would be in trouble. The rest of the story is we are redeemed from the curse of the law!

We are heirs of God, joint heirs with Jesus Christ. His joy is our joy. His joy is not affected by temporal situations. His joy is established by eternal truths—like we are blessed with all spiritual blessings in heavenly places in Christ. Truths bring joy and one definition for joy is having great pleasure.

1 Peter 4:12-13 says *"Beloved, think it not strange concerning the fiery trial which is to try you, as though some strange thing happened unto you: But rejoice,*

inasmuch as ye are partakers of Christ's sufferings; that, when his glory shall be revealed, ye may be glad also with exceeding joy." It almost seems like a contradiction of terms to say to rejoice in fiery trials, but real joy is not just laughter. Real joy is the satisfaction of knowing something good is happening even when it looks and even feels like something bad is going on. It comes from looking beyond the temporary to the eternal.

In John 15 Jesus is speaking of the parable of the vine. He is telling us that He is the vine and we are the branches. He says in verse 7, *"If ye abide in me, and my words abide in you, ye shall ask what ye will, and it shall be done unto you."* Then in verse 11 he says, *"These things have I spoken unto you, that my joy might remain in you, and that your joy might be full."* God wants us to have a true joy that cannot be taken away. Let's look at Luke 10:17.

Here Jesus is sending the seventy out to the cities that he would eventually go to. He told them, *"And heal the sick that are therein, and say to them, the kingdom of God is come nigh unto you"* (verse 9). When they returned, they were rejoicing that even the devils were subject to them in Jesus name. Then Jesus tells them in verse 20, *"Notwithstanding in this rejoice not, that the spirits are subject unto you; but rather rejoice, because your names are written in heaven."*

I believe Jesus was telling them not to rejoice over

things that could change because the truth is, tomorrow your faith may not be as strong as it was today. But even if it is not, I can rejoice because my name is still written in Heaven. If your joy is in things that are forever settled in heaven then no one or no thing can steal your joy. If you can only rejoice in temporary things then your joy will only be temporary. Thank God for an everlasting joy. The Joy of the Lord is my strength. Do not let anybody steal your joy, you need HIS strength!

7

The Way of War

"There is a way that seemeth right unto a man, but the end thereof is death" (Proverbs 14:12). Many people are wearing themselves out simply trying to feel their way through life. People will not stop long enough to read the directions. The Bible is full of directions for our lives but it cannot help us if we will not read it. It really should not be a big surprise, especially for us men; we are embarrassed or something about asking for directions. We will use up a full tank of gas before we will stop and ask somebody for directions. I was taught somewhere along the line that it was a sign of weakness to read the directions before putting something together. Reading the directions is kind of like admitting that I do not know what I am doing. I am not admitting that; instead, I will take three times longer to put something together or to get to my destination. This may sound silly, but it is the truth.

Well, it may be okay to do this with a bicycle, but when we are continually failing at life, I would think sooner or later we would get a clue. God is the creator of life; He knows the way. In fact, He says in John 14:6 *"I am the way, the truth and the life: no man cometh unto the Father but by me."* It really is not a slap to our ego to ask for directions. In fact, it may save us a whole lot of heartache, as well as headache. The text says there is a way that seems right. We all know things are seldom what they seem. Why are we dead set on finding our own way; trying all of the roads that seem right, first, then when we are worn out and can not enjoy the destination, we give in and ask for directions.

The problem is life is passing us by. We could really be enjoying life; instead, we are determined to explore the ways of death; the ways that lead to death as opposed to ways that lead to life. Proverbs 12:28 says *"In the way of righteousness is life: and in the pathway thereof there is no death."* The ways of death are really the ways of the flesh. Galatians 5:16 says *"This I say then, Walk in the Spirit, and ye shall not fulfill the lust of the flesh. For the flesh lusteth against the Spirit, and the Spirit against the flesh: and these are contrary the one to the other: so that ye cannot do the things that ye would."*

The flesh wars against the Spirit. The Spirit leads to life and the flesh leads to death. Now Paul goes on to say in verses 19-21, *"Now the works of the flesh are manifest, which are these; Adultery, fornication, uncleanness, lasciviousness, Idolatry, witchcraft, hatred, variance, emulations, wrath, strife, seditions, heresies, Envyings, murders, drunkenness, revellings and such like: of the which I tell you before, as I have also told you in time past, that they which do such things shall not inherit the kingdom of God."*

These are the ways of death or at least some of them; death basically means separation. When someone dies in the natural, they are separated from those still living. When we do things like Paul lists here, we separate ourselves from the Spirit of God which literally is the Spirit of life. We are participating in works or death when we separate ourselves from God.

Paul goes on to tell us what the fruits of the Spirit are in verses 22-23. *"But the fruit of the Spirit is love, joy, peace, longsuffering, gentleness, goodness, faith, meekness, temperance: against such there is no law."* These are the ways of life, or the ways that bring life. When we speak evil or negative about someone, we are speaking words of death. Proverbs 18:21 says, *"Death and life are in the power of the tongue, and they that love it shall eat the fruit thereof."* We really do need to be careful how we talk; we can speak words of life, or words of death over people. Galatians also says in chapter 6:7, *"Be not deceived; God is not mocked: for whatsoever a man soweth, that shall he also reap. For he that soweth to his flesh shall of the flesh reap corruption; but he that soweth to the Spirit shall of the Spirit reap life everlasting."*

So when we speak words of life over someone else, we are literally sowing life into them, and when we sow life into others we are also sowing life into ourselves, and we reap that which we sow! Oh yea, it also works the other way too. So let us sow life. It is not only in the words we speak, but it is also in the deeds we do.

Another passage of scripture that goes along the same lines is Proverbs 3:5-6. It says *"Trust in the Lord with all thine heart; and lean not unto thine own understanding. In all thy ways acknowledge him and he shall direct thy paths."* We all have the tendency to want to lean to our own understanding, much like a way that seems right. The thing He is telling us here is to acknowledge the Lord and trust in Him. By trusting in the Lord and not leaning to our own understanding, we are assuring ourselves of the best possible way of life. He knows our path of life. He can take us to our destiny without all of the detours.

If we will only listen to the voice of the Lord, and follow His plan, life truly will be worth living. You see, there really is no greater feeling in this world than to know that you are fulfilling your destiny. You are accomplishing what you were actually put here to do; this really is possible. I know some of you may be thinking that it is too late, you have already wasted too many years, but I believe this is what the Bible is talking about in Joel 2:25 when He said that He will *"...restore to you the years that the locust hath eaten, the cankerworm, and the caterpillar, and the palmerworm...."*

We may have wasted some years but our willingness to repent and ask for forgiveness will bring the favor of God back into our lives, and He can restore what was stolen from us, even if we were to blame. God does not hold grudges, God forgives and restores! We just waste a lot of time and energy by not listening to God in the first place. I guess this is why we are so tired.

War and Prayer

P reviously I was reading from Ephesians chapter 6 about the weapons of our warfare. I stopped a little bit too soon. Verse 18 of this chapter says, *"Praying always with all prayer and supplication in the spirit, and watching thereunto with all perseverance and supplication for all saints."*

Prayer is another powerful weapon at our disposal. Many times, it is overlooked. We really do not seem to appreciate how powerful prayer can be. I may have touched on that a little, but I want to drive home the importance of a strong prayer life. I am really not referring to the ministry of intercession; that is something else altogether, but I am talking about the average Christian, walking in his or her calling, must know how to pray.

Once again, let me emphasize it is not to be a ritual or a law; it is simply talking with the Father. Jesus said in Matthew 23:14, *"Woe unto you, scribes and Pharisees, hypocrites! for ye devour widows' houses, and for a pretence make long prayer: therefore ye shall receive the greater damnation."* Praying long prayer to show people that you can pray long prayers does not impress God. It did not impress Jesus back then and it does not impress Him now.

He wants you to talk to Him; tell Him how you feel; not for show. James Chapter 5 verse 16 tells us *"Confess your faults one to another, and pray one for another, that ye may be healed. The effectual fervent prayer of a righteous man availeth much."* The next two verses illustrate this for us. *"Elias was a man subject to like passions as we are, and he prayed earnestly that it might not rain: and it rained not on the earth by the space of three years and six months. And he prayed again, and the heaven gave rain, and the earth brought forth her fruit."*

One man prayed for it not to rain and it did not rain for three years and six months; he prayed again and it rained. What power! The thing we must realize is this was not Elijah's idea. He was speaking, through prayer, what God had told him to say. He did not do this on his own; He was obedient to the word of the Lord. He was the instrument that God used to stop and start the rain.

You see, it is the plan of God to use man to speak things into existence in this natural realm; the things that God wants done. Remember Abraham according to Romans 4:17 *"(As it is written, I have made thee a father of many nations,) before him whom he believed, even God,*

*who quickeneth the dead, and calleth those things which be
not as though they were. Who against hope believed in
hope, that he might become the father of many nations,
according to that which was spoken, So shall thy seed be."*

Now again, we need to understand that Abraham
only did what he was told, and because he did, he was
called (chosen) to be the father of many nations. Simply
put, he heard God, and obeyed and reaped the benefits.
This is really how God works. God is not looking for
people who will make God look good. God is looking
for people who will simply obey! The problem is God's
ways are not our ways, so when He tells you something,
it takes faith to do it.

Noah will be remembered throughout history for
building a boat, nowhere near water, and it was too big
to move. What a fool people thought him to be, but I
am glad, aren't you? If he had not obeyed, we probably
would not be here today. You may be wondering what
this has to do with prayer, but it was in their prayer
time where they received their instructions, by following
those instructions they were used by God to change or
impact (if you will) the course of history. God is not
looking for great men, he is looking for men or women
with a great God!

I am saying this because I see so many people
wanting to make their mark on society by doing
seemingly great things, when in reality all they are doing

is impressing a few folk. They are not impressing God. Faith impresses God. Abraham was chosen to be the father of many nations because he believed God when it looked impossible. It does not record Abraham's mistake here but we know he really messed up by trying to help God by having a son with his handmaiden. Evidently God did not hold it against him; he still used him. The point I want us to get is while spending time with God, God told him to do something, he did it and will be forever remembered for it. He did not think it up, God did.

Going back to the scripture in James, *"The effectual fervent prayer of a righteous man availeth much."* Much happens when people pray; nothing happens when they do not. He did not say how long you had to pray. He said to pray; 1 Thessalonians 5:17 says to *"pray without ceasing."* Always have a prayer on your heart. I believe we should have a running conversation with God, just talk to Him, all day, and let Him talk to you. You might be surprised at what He says. Speaking on the subject of prayer, it would be unforgivable not to mention 2 Chronicles 7:14. Let's begin at verse 12, *"And the Lord appeared to Solomon by night, and said unto him, I have heard thy prayer, and have chosen this place to myself for an house of sacrifice. If I shut up heaven that there be no rain, or if I command the locusts to devour the land, or if I send pestilence among my people; If my people, which are called by my name, shall humble themselves, and pray, and seek my face, and turn from their wicked ways; then will I hear from heaven, and will forgive their sin, and will heal their land."*

God is speaking to Solomon, and giving him authority to literally turn back the hand of God, because Solomon prayed. Authority can only be given to people who understand authority. Solomon was the greatest king that ever lived, (aside from the King of Kings) and yet Solomon submitted to authority. Most men in Solomon's place would not even think about God. He had everything a man could want, he needed nothing.

You talk about extreme, Solomon had it, but he knew without God he still had nothing. Solomon was also known for his wisdom. In all his wisdom he prayed. Are we wiser than Solomon? If Solomon needed to pray, do we?

How does all of this talk about prayer make the battle any easier. It almost sounds like more work. Part of the reason we do not read and pray is because we are too busy already. How is this going to help? I honestly believe we literally waste years of our lives by not getting our orders from headquarters before we go to battle.

I am reminded of a man who was really going through some rough times. It seemed like everything was falling apart around him. His health, his family, and his finances. He asked me if I had any suggestions for him and his situation. I told him that I did not readily know the answer to his situation, but if he would seek God, God had the answer. He said it was too much of a battle to pray. He did not want to fight anymore, he was tired of fighting.

There are so many people in this same situation but the answer is not in running away. We should be running to God, He not only has the answer, He is the answer! I have seen God change a person's entire life with one word. The reason we are so tired of fighting is because we are doing the fighting. It is really God's battle, not ours!

Since we are discussing prayer, something needs to be thought about or at least considered. That is, how we pray and what we pray for. First, let's look at how Jesus said to pray. In Matthew 6, Jesus is giving instructions on how to pray. In verse 5 he tells us not to pray like the hypocrites, who love to pray standing in the synagogues and on the street corners so they can be seen. He said they have their reward. They were not praying to get anything from God, they were praying to impress men. Then Jesus says when you pray, enter into the closet and when you have shut the door, pray to the Father which is in secret. And then the Father which sees you in secret will reward you openly. Then he says in verse 7, *"use not vain repetitions, as the heathen do, for they think that they shall be heard for their much speaking."* He said to not be like them *"for your Father knoweth what things you have need of, before you ask*

Him."

Now in verse 9 Jesus begins to teach us how to pray. Many people call this the Lord's prayer. I do not think this was the Lord's prayer but a model prayer. One reason is because he said, *"After this manner therefore pray ye."* Another reason I do not believe this is the Lord's prayer is because he says to ask for forgiveness of sins. We know that Jesus was not guilty of sin. He was the spotless lamb. Anyway, he says to pray like this, *"Our Father which art in heaven, hallowed by thy name. Thy kingdom come, thy will be done in earth as it is in heaven. Give us this day our daily bread, And forgive us our debts as we forgive our debtors. And lead us not into temptation but deliver us from evil: For thine is the kingdom, and the power and the glory, for ever. Amen."*

I am not going to spend a lot of time here dissecting this passage, maybe in another book, but I do want us to see that the pattern is to see the kingdom first as it says in verse 33 of the Matthew 6. Then all of these things we need will be taken care of. Most of our prayers are just wish lists. We are not praying the Father's heart, we are praying ours. When we speak His word into existence and pray His heart, the things He desires will be manifest on the earth. We will see that He knows how to take care of our needs, abundantly beyond our expectations. Ephesians 3:20 says, *"Now unto him that is able to do exceeding abundantly above all that we ask or think, according to the power that worketh in us."* This is God's reward for praying His way!

One other thing I think needs to be addressed are some of the things that we pray for.   Now I am not saying that we should not pray for these things; I am just saying we need to take into consideration how these kinds of prayers are answered. For instance, when we pray for patience; Romans 5:3 tells us that *"tribulation worketh patience."* In other words, tribulation strengthens or helps to build our patience. So when you pray for patience, God grants your request by giving you tribulations.

Another witness to this is found in James beginning in verse 2, *"My brethren, count it all joy when ye fall into divers temptations; Knowing this, that the trying of your faith worketh patience."*

Again, I am not saying not to pray for patience, because patience is a good thing to have.   I am just letting you know the process by which it comes. We live in a microwave society; push a button and "there it is," but God does not operate like a microwave. We just want someone to lay hands on us and give us patience, or whatever else it is we want, but the truth is, this is not always how it works.

Now I am not against laying on of hands. I do it myself, but we must realize some of the stuff that we go through is not because God is mad at us or because we have sinned again. It may be that our prayers are being answered. God is working something into our lives that only comes through experience, or He might be working something out of our lives, either way it can be a good thing!

Some people work hard and some people work smart. Some pray hard and some pray smart. It really is your choice. In any case, pray. Prayer not only changes things, it also changes you!

The Warfare and The Church

I would like to go back to something I mentioned earlier in the first chapter. I made the statement that the battle between the Israelites and Philistines was a picture of the church. The church is on one mountain and the enemy is on another, and there is a valley between them. In scripture, mountains represent Kingdoms. Colossians 1:13 talks about the Lord *"who hath delivered us from the power of darkness, and hath translated us into the kingdom of his dear Son."* He has delivered us from the power or kingdom of darkness and translated us into His kingdom.

When we think of being translated, we think of being taken from one place and put in another, but in reality, being translated is to be changed as we do when we translate languages. We change the words so someone else can understand. God changes us so the world can better understand Him. I was moved from one kingdom to another, but I did not have to go anywhere!

We are still picturing the church on one mountain and the world on another and that is alright for the purpose of understanding. The reality is, it is not the way it is supposed to be. You see, the problem the Jews (who were the church of that day) had with Jesus is that he did not distinguish himself from the sinner like they thought he should. The Bible says Jesus was a friend of the sinner. He did not stay up on the mountain, He came down where they were. In fact, He really did not see them as the enemy; He saw them as friends.

This, in my opinion, is one of the big mistakes we have made in the church. We are so worried about being brought down that we are afraid to get too involved with them. Jesus was not too worried; He got right down there with them. He knew who He was and was not even tempted to be like them because He knew they were just people who had missed the mark and He knew He could help them. The sinner did not have anything He needed, but He had everything they needed. He was not going to hold back anything.

Jesus had no problem with the sinner. His biggest challenge was the church system of the day. He spoke kindness to the sinner and rebuke to the religious crowd. We will never have the impact that Jesus had as long as we see ourselves on different mountains. Jesus, like David, was willing to climb down off the mountain and meet the enemy face to face. Keep in mind, the person we are looking at, is not the enemy. The enemy is the spirit or force that is driving them. This is why He said we do not fight against flesh and blood, but against principalities, powers, and spiritual wickedness in high places.

The highest place in your body is your mind. When spiritual wickedness gets in our mind, it is time for a renewing of the mind. Romans 12:1-2 says *"I beseech you therefore, brethren by the mercies of God, that ye present your bodies a living sacrifice, holy, acceptable unto God, which is your reasonable service. And be not conformed to this world: but be ye transformed by the renewing of your mind, that ye may prove what is that good, and acceptable, and perfect will of God."* There must be a renewing of the mind. Let's look at Philippians 2:5, *"Let this mind be in you, which was also in Christ Jesus."* The Bible also says in 1 Corinthians 2:16, *"For who hath known the mind of the Lord, that he may instruct him? But we have the mind of Christ."* Paul is telling us that we do not have the capability to tell God what to do, but we do have available to us, the mind of Christ.

Paul told the Ephesians in chapter 5 verses 25-26, *"Husbands, love your wives, even as Christ also loved the church, and gave himself for it. That he might sanctify and cleanse it with the washing of water by the word."* So the Bible is telling us that our mind must be washed by the word and we can have the mind of Christ.

We can know the things of God, the will of God.

We can walk on this earth in all that God has planned for us if we will allow ourselves to believe, *"with God all things are possible"* (Matthew 19:26). With a renewed mind that is sanctified (set apart) for God to use, we can overcome anything that might come our way, and we do not have to be overwhelmed by the pressures of the world.

Getting back to Romans 12:2, he said to *"be not conformed to this world but be ye transformed by the renewing of your mind, that ye may prove what is that good, and acceptable, and perfect, will of God."* We do not have to settle for that which is good, or even acceptable, but we can have the perfect will of God. Many are satisfied to dwell in mediocrity but why settle for less when God has provided the best for us? Hebrews 6:1 says *"Therefore leaving the principles of the doctrine of Christ, let us go on unto perfection; not laying again the foundation of repentance from dead works, and of faith toward God."*

Paul is challenging the church to go on to perfection. Many have concluded that nobody is perfect so why try, but the word perfection is really maturity. In other words, the command is to grow up. Continue growing until we are grown.

Another favorite scripture of mine on this subject is Ephesians 4:11-15, *"And he gave some, apostles; and some, prophets; and some, evangelists; and some, pastors and teachers; For the perfecting of the saints, for the work of the ministry, for the edifying of the body of Christ: Till we all come in the unity of the faith, and of the knowledge of the Son of God, unto a perfect man, unto the measure of the stature of the fulness of Christ: That we henceforth be no more children, tossed to and fro, and carried about with every wind of doctrine, by the sleight of men, and cunning craftiness, whereby they lie in wait to deceive; But speaking the truth in love, may grow up into him in all things, which is the head, even Christ."*

Basically, Paul is telling us that the five fold ministry was given to us for the perfecting or maturing of the saints, that we may grow up into him, a perfect or mature man or woman. The reason I have included this in the book is because of the growing process; it can be very trying and as Paul says, being tossed around with every wind of doctrine, by the sleight of men and cunning craftiness. This is, unfortunately, part of the process. And it can wear on you but I am reminded again of the verse in Romans 8 that says, *"For I reckon that the sufferings of this present time are not worthy to be compared with the glory which shall be revealed in us"* (18). In other words, the reward will outweigh the trials. The trials are not worth comparing to the victory that is ours in Christ!

He is also telling us if we will grow, we will not be tossed to and fro and carried about by every wind of doctrine. Notice, he also said by the sleight of men or cunning craftiness of men.   As we mature in Christ, we can see through the ways of men trying to lead us to do things their way and not God's. This will save us a lot of time and energy if we will heed the word of the Lord. Grow!

10

The Warrior and The Warfare

" No man that warreth entangleth himself with the affairs of this life, that he may please him who hath chosen him to be a soldier" (2 Timothy 2:4). In Paul's instructions to Timothy he compares the Christian walk to a soldier in the army. Only in this army, the soldiers are not just volunteers, they are chosen.

Jesus tells us in St. John 15:16 "*Ye have not chosen me, but I have chosen you, and ordained you, that ye should go and bring forth fruit, and that your fruit should remain: that whatsoever ye shall ask of the Father in my name, he may give it you.*" For a long time I thought it was my choice to serve the Lord and though I did choose to follow Him, He had already chosen me, and if you are following Him, it is because He first chose you. Paul repeats this in the book of 2 Thessalonians 2:13, "*But we are bound to give thanks alway to God for you, brethren beloved of the Lord, because God hath from the beginning chosen you to salvation through sanctification of the Spirit and belief of the truth.*"

It is a great pleasure to be chosen of God even from the beginning, but the warning given to us in 2 Timothy was to not get entangled with the things of this world, that we may please Him who hath called us. How do we get tangled up in this world?

One of the first things that comes to my mind is our daily affairs. It is so easy to get caught up in just trying to make it that we forget the reason we are here. Our purpose in life is so much more than building houses or fixing cars or even running corporations. The plan of God is much more important than making money!

I remember many years ago when I first started preaching, one of my first sermons was "God Has a Plan." I took my text from the book of Joshua. Joshua had to take the city of Jericho. He sought the Lord and God gave him a plan. His plan was to have his army to walk around the city one time a day for six days and on the seventh day, walk around seven times. Then, on the last trip around, "shout for the Lord hath given you the city."   They did not have the city yet but God said to shout. When they did, the walls of the city fell and Joshua and his men took the city. This is another one of those orders that just does not make sense, to our natural mind.

But the battle is not limited to natural things, if we are going to win, we must understand this. Spiritual battles will only be won spiritually. The effects will manifest in the natural, but the battle is not limited to natural strategies. Being so entangled with natural things consumes so much of our time and energy that we so easily forget this is a spiritual battle. We need to get spiritual instructions; it will have natural effects and give us many more victories, and bring much joy to our lives. Simple obedience is still the key. Joshua was obedient to the plan of God. He won the battle at Jericho, but in the midst of the battle one of his men gave in to temptation, and took some gold. God had told them not to take anything.

Because of his disobedience when Joshua went to fight the next battle, they ran from the enemy, and it cost many their lives. This is not so far removed from what goes on in our lives. In the heat of the battle we get our eyes off of the Lord and on to the immediate gratification. Our mind tells us "Why wait" when there are so many things that can bring temporary satisfaction. We settle for the temporary and miss out on the eternal reward; not a reward we will some day get in eternity, but a reward that will be eternally beneficial.

2 Corinthians 4:17-18 says *"For our light affliction, which is but for a moment, worketh for us a far more exceeding and eternal weight of glory; While we look not at the things which are seen, but at the things which are not seen: for the things which are seen are temporal; but the things which are not seen are eternal."* The things we work so hard for will one day perish but the things that really matter we seem to take so lightly. The most important is our relationship with our heavenly Father; our relationship with Him is reflected in our relationship with others. 1 John 4:20 says *"If a man say, I love God, and hateth his brother, he is a liar: for he that loveth not his brother whom he hath seen, how can he love God whom*

he hath not seen?"

Relationships are important to God, yet we take them so lightly. This is just one of those unseen things, there are many more. The important thing is not getting caught up in everyday things and letting the important things go by. Another way to keep from getting so entangled with the affairs of this life, and one which will also bring a person closer to the Lord, is to get involved in the work of the Lord, not just in your local church, but outside the church. One of the best ways to appreciate what you have is to get involved in missions. Reach out to the world. I never realized how blessed we were here in America until I went to a third world nation. Not only that, but to see the hunger that people have for God, is life-changing. You will never see things the same again. If you really want to be a soldier for the Lord, get out of your comfort zone. Many can not go overseas but you can get involved in feeding the homeless, or visiting shut-ins.

There is something that everyone can do. Not only will you be helping others, it will help you too. One of our biggest hang ups is self-centeredness. We think everything should revolve around us. One of the greatest revelations I received was when the Lord let me know that my life "is not about me." Everything does not need to bring attention my way. It is about Christ being revealed, not flesh.

Paul told the church in Galatians 4:19, *"My little children, of whom I travail in birth again until Christ be formed in you."* When Christ is revealed in you, people will no longer see you or your personality, but His. Our concerns will be His concerns. He is concerned about reaching people, here and abroad. Remember the Great Commission, *"Go ye therefore, and teach (make disciples) all nations, baptizing them in the name of the Father, and of the Son, and of the Holy Ghost"* (Matthew 28:19). If you cannot go, help someone who can. By doing so, you will get your focus off of yourself, help someone else, and you will grow up and begin revealing the Christ in you.

"Wherefore seeing we also are compassed about with so great a cloud of witnesses, let us lay aside every weight, and the sin which doth so easily beset us, and let us run with patience the race that is set before us, Looking unto Jesus the author and finisher of our faith; who for the joy that was set before him endured the cross, despising the shame, and is set down at the right hand of the throne of God. For consider him that endured such contradiction of sinners against himself, lest ye be wearied and faint in your minds" (Hebrews 12:1-3).

This word of the Lord to the Hebrews was realizing that so many people are watching, 'let's be careful.' Let us put away the things in our life that would hinder us from reaching our destiny. Jesus knew His destiny was the cross. Anything that would deter Him from achieving that destiny was considered an enemy. Anything, whether it be something in your life or something that affects you from without, is your enemy, especially if it keeps you from fulfilling God's call on your life.

He said to lay aside those things that negatively influence you, those things that weigh you down. It may be doctrines or ideologies that have been handed down to you that are keeping you from moving on in the things of God.

Looking at the life of Jesus, how tempting it must have been to want to stay a little while longer, do a few more good things, teach a few more lessons just to make sure they really got the message, because sometimes it just did not look like the disciples were getting it. But there was a time appointed and it had to be according to the plan of the ages. It did look like they needed him to hang around a little while longer, I mean he was just 33 years old. You see, this is the kind of thinking that hinders the work of God; the weight that so easily besets us, trying to reason with our minds the plan of God. The Bible also tells us that obedience is better than sacrifice.

Let's look at verse 3 again in the Amplified Bible. *"Just think of him who endured from sinners such grievous opposition and better hostility against himself (reckon up and consider it all in comparison with your trials) so that you may not grow weary or exhausted, losing heart and relaxing and fainting in your minds."* In other words, when it looks like you are being stretched beyond your capabilities and you just do not know if you can go on, stop and think about what Jesus went through. Most of our trials are mild in comparison to his. So we have

to give up some things we are probably better off
without anyway. I am not talking about giving up
pleasures as much as I am talking about giving up our
plans.

I remember when I was first called into the ministry,
I was in a really good denomination, the Lord had led
me in another direction, but I am still thankful for all
that people did for me. God was leading me to go to
this church but I had told my wife that I would go
anywhere but there. You see, it was my home church;
I was raised in that church. Those people knew me as
little Randy, they would never accept me as Pastor Randy.
"No, anywhere but there." Well, obviously God did
not hear, or at least He did not seem to care about my
opinion. He would not leave me alone about it. The
people from the church were calling, nothing else
seemed to be working out. But I still was not the least
bit interested in going back there. Finally, I began to
get tired of having no peace. I really did not think that
it would work out, so why bother? But God simply
would not leave me alone.

The effects of our disobedience were beginning to
affect us, even our relationship was being tried.
Finally, we decided something had to be done. We
began praying one night and literally we prayed all night.
I am not trying to sound super spiritual; we were just
that desperate to find relief. After praying all night
long we decided if God was really wanting us to go there,
he would take away my job. I thought things were going
pretty good at work so it seemed like a good fleece. The

very next morning when I got in the truck with my co-worker, the first thing he said was "today is the day." He did not have to say another word, though it was unexpected, I knew it was time to move.

Now my problem was not only that I did not want to go there, it was that I had other plans that really seemed to make more sense. It was not long after we arrived there when God began showing us this really was His plan. We saw many people saved and lives changed. Thank God. This is why Jesus prayed not my will, but thine be done. Our will is one of the hardest things to give up, but it is one of the biggest things that gets in the way. Oh, it is easy to repeat the prayer, but to mean it is a different story. We will find that God's will is always the best. Psalm 27:11 says *"Teach me thy way O Lord, and lead me in a plain path, because of mine enemies."* This is a prayer of David as King, that God would teach him His ways and lead him in a plain path.

My prayer is that our path be plain, not only so we can find it and stay in it, but make it not so complicated. It does not have to be a path that elevates us above others or makes us look sophisticated, just a plain path will do.

Another scripture that we must look at concerning this subject is Psalm 119:105. *"Thy word is a lamp unto my feet, and a light unto my path."* David knew the word of the Lord would show him the way. It really is a light given that we may know the next step. By knowing the word and by hearing the word and obeying the word, life is rewarding. It is not always easier, but it is worth living.

11

Why War?

Proverbs has much to say on this subject of "why is it so hard?" One of these passages is found in Proverbs 13, beginning in verse 12. *"Hope deferred maketh the heart sick: but when the desire cometh, it is a tree of life. Whoso despiseth the word shall be destroyed: but he that feareth the commandment shall be rewarded. The law of the wise is a fountain of life, to depart from the snares of death. Good understanding giveth favour: but the way of transgressors is hard."* A transgressor is someone who knows the law or who has heard the instruction and chooses not to obey.

Referring back to my experience earlier, I was a transgressor and my way was hard, but I was not necessarily sinning; I was just not being obedient. Many people have made life hard simply by not doing what they know they should be doing. Many people are miserable, going from relationship to relationship, looking for love in all of the wrong places. They cannot find happiness because happiness is not an end in itself. Happiness is the result of finding purpose in life. Find your place and you will find happiness!

When speaking of happiness, I think of the Beatitudes in Matthew, chapter 5, *"Blessed are they which do hunger and thirst after righteousness: for they shall be filled. Blessed are the pure in heart: for they shall see God."* Another word for blessed is happy. Those who are hungry and thirsty for righteousness will be filled and made happy. Happiness comes as a result of the desires of being fulfilled.

Psalm 37:4-5 says *"Delight thyself also in the Lord: and he shall give thee the desires of thine heart. Commit thy way unto the Lord; trust also in him; and he shall bring it to pass."* Delight means to give great pleasure to, or enjoy. So we are to enjoy ourselves in the Lord. And he will give us the desires of our heart. It sounds like he wants us to be happy. If we are happy and our desires are being met by the Lord, then why do we make the Christian walk seem so hard. It really is the only way to go.

Living for the Lord is a joy, not a burden. We really should be the happiest people on earth. Many people are living in this place of deferred hope and their hearts are sick. The heart is the seat of our emotions or feelings. When your heart is sick, nothing will satisfy. Deferred hope is a hope that is put off, and hope that cannot be attained really is not hope at all. Then He said when the desired thing does come, it is a tree of life. We first hear of the Tree of Life in the Garden of Eden. Even then, man chose to eat of the Tree of Knowledge of Good and

Evil, deferring Hope.

Later, we learn that Jesus Christ was the Tree of Life and whosoever will, may come and partake once again but many still choose to defer this hope. People still want to eat from the tree of knowledge instead. It is no wonder most people still have a sick heart.

We find another place in scripture that deals with spiritual sickness. It is in 1 Corinthians 11:30 it says *"For this cause many are weak and sickly among you, and many sleep."* The context of this passage is the Apostle Paul teaching on the Lord's Supper. Now, I am not saying this sacrament should not be practiced literally. I am saying, however, there is a whole lot more to it than just eating bread and drinking juice.

When Jesus took the bread, he said this is my body. In the next chapter Paul tells us that ye are the body of Christ. He told us to take and eat. To eat, in a spiritual sense would be to partake of one another's fruit which we read about earlier—it is love, peace, joy, gentleness, meekness, and so on. We need to understand that Paul was not telling us to partake of a natural bread, but we need to partake of the fruit which comes from our brothers and sisters, in the spiritual body of Christ. Then he said to partake of the cup which is the new testament in my blood (1 Corinthians 11:25). The new testament or new covenant is a blood covenant. When we take part in the covenant we are agreeing to do our part.

A covenant is an agreement between two parties. It is only as good as the word of those making the covenant.

We know that God has been faithful in doing His part. If there is any problem with the covenant, it is on our part. This is why he says in 27-30, *"Wherefore whosoever shall eat this bread, and drink this cup of the Lord, unworthily, shall be guilty of the body and blood of the Lord. But let a man examine himself, and so let him eat of the bread and drink of that cup. For he that eateth and drinketh unworthily, eateth and drinketh damnation to himself, not discerning the Lord's body. For this cause many are weak and sickly among you and many sleep."*

I believe this is the reason we find so many weak Christians. I am talking about spiritually weak; unable to do the works of the Lord. A strong Christian is supposed to be able to cast out demons, heal the sick, raise the dead. This really should be the norm for Christians. I know this sounds far fetched for many, but remember what Jesus said in John 14:12, *"Verily, verily, I say unto you, He that believeth on me, the works that I do shall he do also; and greater works than these shall he do; because I go unto my Father."*

I am convinced the reason the majority of the church does not walk in this kind of power is because we do not discern the Lord's body and we do not keep our end of the covenant. I really do not believe it is because we drink grape juice or eat wafers without asking for forgiveness first. This really is more serious.

We discern the Lord's body by understanding who the body is and by giving proper respect to the members of His body. You would not intentionally hurt your own body. I have hit my thumb with a hammer before and I promise I did not mean to, nor did I enjoy it.

We should feel the same way about the body of Christ. We are all members of the same body. Paul deals with this in the twelfth chapter of 1 Corinthians. I will not attempt to get into that here, but please understand me, I am not saying we should not have communion, it is up to you or your pastor. I am saying we should have communion with the Father through his body, the church. The church is more than one local body. It is the corporate body, made up of every born again believer, regardless of their affiliation. If they are part of his body, then they are part of your body and you must discern the Lord's body and you must keep the covenant written in his blood.

Now the question arises, what is the covenant and what is our part? Let's look at Hebrews 8:10. *"For this is the covenant that I will make with the house of Israel after those days, saith the Lord; I will put my laws into their mind, and write them in their hearts: and I will be to them a God, and they shall be to me a people."* In other words, God is saying to us that he did his part by buying us back from sin, redeeming us and we will have done our part by walking out His plan here on Earth. He will help us to do this by putting it in our hearts and minds.

This has always been the plan of God for man to walk in the fulness of Christ, to be not only what Adam was when he fell, but to be what Adam could have been if he had continued on. I think this is so exciting to know that it is still possible, and we have God's word that He will do it in us if we will just believe, and let Him.

You may be wondering how I got all of that from one verse, but it is just a synopsis of what is being taught in the whole book of Hebrews. If you want to understand it better, study the book of Hebrews. There are a couple more things I think we need to look at before I finish this book. One is in the book of Luke, chapter 4, beginning in verse 18, *"The Spirit of the Lord is upon me, because he hath anointed me to preach the gospel to the poor; he hath sent me to heal the brokenhearted, to preach deliverance to the captives, and recovering of sight to the blind, to set at liberty them that are bruised, (19) To preach the acceptable year of the Lord."* Then it says He closed the book and all eyes were on Him and He said to them, *"This day is this scripture fulfilled in your ears."*

When Jesus was saying all of this, He was not out in the streets or even in the bars or prisons; He was in the church. He was telling them that He came to set the captives free, and today I am setting you free. You see, there are so many sitting in the four walls of the church that are so bound up in religion and tradition that Jesus said I am sent to you. He said that He was sent to preach the gospel to the poor.

The gospel is the good news. Someone said that good news to a poor person is that they are not poor any more. If you can believe, you will receive. Another scripture says that *"According to your faith, be it unto you"* (Matthew 9:29). Ephesians 3:20 says, *"Now unto him that is able to do exceeding abundantly above all that we ask or think, according to the power that worketh in us."* I am saying all of this to help us realize that God wants to bless us and has already blessed us so that we are not poor, if we do not have a dime to our name, we are rich in Christ Jesus. If we can exercise our faith we can access all of heaven. Ephesians 1:3 says *"Blessed be the God and Father of our Lord Jesus Christ, who hath blessed us with all spiritual blessings in heavenly places in Christ."* Hath is past tense; the blessings have already been given; we are not poor.

The same can be said for the rest of the message that Jesus was preaching. He was sent to heal the broken-hearted, preach deliverance to the captives. All of these things have already been taken care of in Jesus Christ. We, as the church, should no longer need to be healed of broken hearts or delivered from captivity.

The truth is we need to be like Christ and be delivering others. He also said to recover sight to the blind. We know that we have the ability in Christ to heal literally, but He is not just talking about literal blindness. Going to Ephesians, chapter one again, verse 18, it says *"The eyes of your understanding being enlightened; that ye may know what is the hope of his calling, and what the riches of the glory of his inheritance in the saints."*

We are in need of spiritual enlightening that we may be able to see what God has prepared for those that love Him. 1 Corinthians 2:9 says *"But as it is written, Eye hath not seen, nor ear heard, neither have entered into the heart of man, the things which God hath prepared for them that love him."* Many times we stop reading there, but the next verse says, *"But God hath revealed them unto us by his Spirit: for the Spirit searcheth all things, yea, the deep things of God."*

At one time, man did not know what God had prepared for him, but now it has been revealed and we can know. These things are not something to be had someday in the future, but are available to us now. God is not a God of the future, He is the God of now! Today is the day of salvation, the Bible says. He told Moses "That I am that I am" not the "I will be." He will still be God in the future, but He does not want us living in the future; He wants us to tap into the heavenlies and access our inheritance.

The inheritance is available to the heirs after the giver dies, not after the receiver dies. That would not work too well, would it? Then he said to set at liberty them that are bruised. Many in the church and in the world are tired of being knocked around by the system. Every so often someone will have enough and stand up and take action; almost every time people are set free from some kind of abuse because of it.

This is what Jesus was doing for us; He was tired of people being pushed around. He stood up and settled the score. We are free from the bondages of sin, the guilt and condemnation that comes with it. Romans 8:1 says *"There is therefore now no condemnation to them which are in Christ Jesus, who walk not after the flesh, but after the Spirit."* I am glad he said "now."

Next, he said that he was sent to preach the acceptable year of the Lord. Whenever this message is preached, it is the acceptable year of the Lord; not just a good time to accept Him as Lord and Savior, which we should do, but to accept the work that He did for us and to accept the responsibility to spread the good news to others.

You may be thinking this sounds like too much. You were supposed to be helping me, not giving me more work to do. I am reminded of the saying about losing yourself in your work. There really is no better way to lose yourself than in the work of the Lord. You will lose your identity and find His. He will give you strength which you will not believe. This really is a good thing!

12

Winning the War

In the book of Daniel, chapter 7:25, it says that one of the strategies of the enemy is to wear out the saints of the most High. His strategy has not changed much in all these years. When a person gets wore down, they do not think right; they get irritable, they will say things they normally would not say, or do things they normally would not do. 2 Corinthians 2:11 says *"Lest Satan should get an advantage of us; for we are not ignorant of his devices."*

Paul said he was not ignorant of Satan's devices, but it does not mean that we are not. We will quote scripture sometimes and think it becomes true for us. It can become true for us, but not just because we can quote it. We truly must become aware of his devices. Devices like, "He wants to wear out the saints."

Our victory comes from being aware of these strategies and not letting them work on us. Do not let him wear you out. Find your pace and run at your pace. Do not let anyone set your pace for you. In 1 Corinthians 9:24, Paul says *"Know ye not that they which* run in a race run all, but one receiveth the prize? So run, that ye may obtain." Then in verse 26 he says "I therefore so run, not as uncertainly, so fight I, not as one that beateth the air: (verse 27). But I keep under my body, and bring it into subjection: lest that by any means, when I have preached to others, I myself should be a castaway." Paul is speaking of the discipline it takes to be a serious runner or a boxer. Runners participate with the goal of winning the prize. We also have a prize waiting. Philippians 3:14 says "I press toward the mark for the prize of the high calling of God in Christ Jesus." We have something to look forward to. But we must "run with patience the race that is set before us" (Hebrews 12:1).

In other words, whatever it is you want to do in life, you need to sit down and figure out how you are going to accomplish it. Have a plan and stick to it. Do not allow yourself to be distracted by things that seem important. Stick to the plan, it will take you where you want to go.

In the Christian walk we call our enemy the devil. He comes in many shapes and sizes, but his goal is always the same, stop the Christian. The thing we must remember is that the devil was defeated at Calvary. Colossians 2:13-15 says "And you, being dead in your sins and the uncircumcision of your flesh, hath he quickened together with him, having forgiven you all trespasses; Blotting out the handwriting of ordinances that was against us, which was contrary to us, and took it out of the way, *nailing it to the cross; And having spoiled principalities and powers, he made a shew of them openly, triumphing over them in it."* In other words, He took care of the devil. Thank God. The devil is defeated. Our problem is us, our own mind; our lack of dedication and discipline. If we do not succeed, it is not the devil's fault. It is ours. I know we do not like to think like this, and some may really get mad at me now, but it will not change the truth.

I am convinced that we can do this. We can be all that God has called us to be. There is no one or nothing big enough to stop us, if we let God be God in us. He will prevail. We cannot get wore out fighting useless battles.

The battle truly is the Lord's and with Him you cannot fail!